Plastic Doesn't Grow From the Ground

Adapted By: Noah River

Illustrated By: Maryam

Medina House
publishing

Medina House
publishing

www.medinahouse.org
170 Manhattan Ave, PO Box 63
New York 14215
contact@medinahouse.org

Hello Friends,
As Bro and Kro, we would like to thank all of our great readers and supporters! It wouldn't be possible to have so much fun without you during our exciting adventures. Thank you for joining us!

CONTENTS

v

CHAPTER 1

LET'S GO ON A HIKE BRO

One day Bro received a call from his best friend Kro.

Bro answered the call: Asalamu Alaykum Kro, how's it going?

Kro said: Wa Alaykum Salam Bro, I hope I'm not disturbing you?

Bro said: As if you can disturb me!

Kro said: I was wondering

if you could visit me, so we could go on a hike at this place I've just discovered? I bet you would like it!

Bro said: That sounds DOPE MAN! It's been a long time since we have seen each other.

Let me first ask my parents, and then I will call Buraq InshAllah.

Kro said: Alright then, see you in a bit, Asalamu Alaykum Bro...

Bro said: Let's see if I can make it there before you, Asalamu Alaykum...

Bro ran as fast as he can to ask his parents' for permission. After his quick chat with his parents' he thought giving Kro a present would be a good idea. Bro started thinking out loud "Maybe I should give him one of my favorite books about animals". He

grabbed his book from his room immediately and put it in to his backpack. He was now ready to call his teleporting horse, Buraq. He said: Asalamu Alaykum Buraq! Can you please give me a ride, I am ready to go?
Buraq immediately appeared shining with his long, beautiful hair and he was very tall in height. After Bro asked Buraq if he can take him to Siirt-Bagdat (the birth place of Sa- lahuddin Ayyubi), and he took him there in a flash light. Kro saw Bro and said: Hey Bro I am here. Thank you for coming.

4

Bro said: I hope I didn't keep you waiting?"No" said Kro. "I just arrived too".
Bro and Kro started hiking on top of the valleys of Siirt. Bro was so impressed with the nature around him, he even forgot to give Kro his gift.
Bro said: Woww dude, this place is a piece of heaven!!

SubhanAllah!!! It's one of the many beautiful creations of Allah (SWT)!

Kro said: Yeah indeed, Allah (SWT) has decorated the earth in the best way...

Kro continued: If only it wasn't polluted like this. He pointed at the plastic trash all over the place.

CHAPTER 2

PLASTIC DOESN'T GROW FROM THE GROUND

Bro said: I didn't know that you could grow plastic from the ground like this. (He laughed..)
Kro smiled and said: I didn't know that either. Don't worry Bro, I brought this trash bag with me. Kro started picking up the garbage around him.

Bro was so surprised, he said: Hey Kro, are you out of your mind? This would take forever! There is no way you can pick them up all.

Kro said: You might be right, I may not finish it all at once but you know, intention matters, so I will try my best man.

Bro said: Yes, you are right! My mother once told me this hadith: "Verily actions are judged by intentions ".

Kro said: Yeah indeed, Allah (SWT)
has decorated the earth in the best way...

Kro said: What does that mean? Bro said: Allah (SWT) cares about our intentions. Even if you don't end up achieving what you intend to do, Allah (SWT) will reward you.
Kro said: Really? That's a very good deal! It's like a present from Allah (SWT) to us..
Bro suddenly remembered the gift he brought in his backpack and

said: Speaking of presents I
got a present for you.
Bro handed over the book to
Kro. Kro was very surprised
by Bro's gift.
He said: "Oh my God, I love
it! I really enjoy animals and
learning about them. Thank
you very much for your gift."
He continued: By the way, do
you know what my favorite
animal is?
Bro said: Is it a cheetah?
Because that's my favorite
one..
Kro said: I love cheetahs too,
but my favorite one

is panda. I just think we have a lot of things in common with them...

He continued: We should definitely come back here tomorrow Bro. There is a lot more to see. I haveto show you the waterfalls and the cave.

Bro said: Yeah definitely, that's a great idea. It's a sleepover then!

They continued talking about animals on their way back home. After they arrived, they made wudhu and prayed maghrib and ran to the kitchen to enjoy the delicious dinner Kro's mom prepared. They enjoyed the rest of the night, prayed Isha and went to bed.

CHAPTER 3

THE STORY OF THE CAVE

In the morning after a beautiful breakfast, they went to the falls, and after an hour they decided to head to the cave.
When Kro saw the cave, he remembered the story his father told him about the Prophet,

Muhammad(SAW).

He said: Hey Bro, do you remember the story about the cave. There was a time when Prophet Muhammad(SAW) neeed to hide from his enemies and took refuge in a cave. While they were hiding, the spiders wove their web to the entrance of the cave and the pigeons followed them by making a nest on top of the web. This led them to

think that the cave was abandoned for a very long time, so they left. My father told me this is the reason why spiders are his favorite animals.

Bro said: Wow! That must be the reason why my mother's favorite animal is pigeon.

Kro said: Maybe the pigeons and spiders are very close friends, just like us.

After they left the cave, they headed to the hiking spot that they went to the day before.

As they were walking, they noticed the place had trash all over again.

Kro said: Man! I'm shocked at the way people are motivated to polluting the environment. Let's see who's more motivated!

He started picking up the plastic bottles and trash around him. Bro was lost in

his thoughts.

Kro looked at Bro and teased him saying: These plastics are not going to pick themselves up, you know that right!!

Bro laughed and said: HAHA, that was a good one, but I think we can do better than this, InshaAllah.

Kro asked: What do you mean?

Bro explained: Why don't we go home and make some posters? Maybe

that would help us with our mission.

Kro said: Now you're talking!! That sounds like a plan to me buddy.

Bro and Kro went back home without wasting time and started making posters. They attached their posters to wooden sticks. They couldn't wait for the next day, so they rushed back to the hiking spot and put up the posters in places where everybody can see.

After a tiring day, they finally decided to go home.

CHAPTER 4

IT WORKED!

The next day, Kro woke up very early because of his excitement, he shook Bro to wake him up and said "Hey BROO, are you planning to spend the rest of your life in that bed you sleepy head!?". Bro said: You know it's still 2 am where I live my muslim brother...

Kro said: Don't you want to go and check if our plan worked!?
Bro replied with his eyes barely opened : Yeah, I'm dying to see. (He yawned)
As soon as their conversation was over, they went to the hiking spot.
When they arrived Bro said: Man, I told you it was gonna work. We did it Alhamdulillah!
Kro said : We did, right? How did this even happen?

Bro said: Did you forget the hadith you told me? All that matters is our intentions. We take a step forward, try our best and leave the rest to Allah(SWT).

Kro said: I am amazed at how fast you are learning Bro.
Bro said: That's because I have such a terrific teacher like you.
They high fived and laughed...

MISSION ACCOMPLISHED!

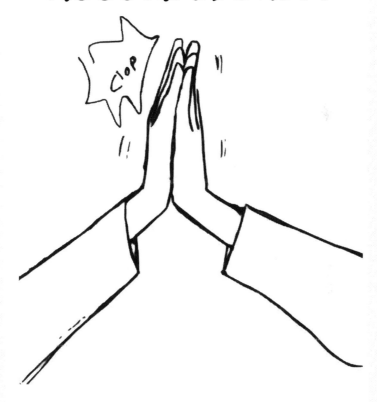

Made in the USA
Middletown, DE
24 October 2023

41360033R00015